+HF5415 .S555

Short Marketing Cases

Kenneth Simmonds

*Professor of Marketing & International Business,
London Business School*

Philip Allan

First published 1987 by
PHILIP ALLAN PUBLISHERS LIMITED
MARKET PLACE
DEDDINGTON
OXFORD OX5 4SE

© Kenneth Simmonds, 1987

All rights reserved. No part of this publication may be reproduced, stored in a retrieval system, or transmitted, in any form or by any means, electronic, mechanical, photocopying, recording or otherwise, without the prior permission of the publishers and the original copyright holders.

British Library Cataloguing in Publication Data

Simmonds, Kenneth
   Short marketing cases.
   1. Marketing—Case studies
   I. Title
   658.8′00722   HF5415

ISBN 0-86003-544-1
ISBN 0-86003-646-4 Pbk

Set in Compugraphic Paladium 11/13 by MHL Typesetting Ltd, Coventry
Printed in Great Britain by Bocardo Press Ltd, Oxford

The owner of the copyright in these cases
is Professor Kenneth Simmonds, of the London
Business School. The cases may NOT be
reproduced for teaching or any other purpose.
This book is available in an inexpensive
paperback version specifically for use by
students.

Contents

Introduction 1

Consumer Motivation and the Marketing Mix

1 The Mousetrap 5

2 Leisure Time Ice 6

3 Josiah Doncaster Ltd 10

Market Measurement and Research

4 Ampex Videocassette Tapes 19

5 Chez Nouveau Furnishings 22

6 Dornbusch Corporation 24

Determining Product Features

7 Waste Water 29

8 Graham's Groceries Ltd 31

9 Ansafone Corporation 33

Distribution

10 Chalfont Bedspreads 43

11 Integrated Offices Ltd   45

12 Metropolitan National Bank Ltd   47

13 Aigle Engineering   49

Promotion

14 Agency 5   55

15 A Line from Sally   57

16 YTS, IBM and Saatchi   64

Pricing

17 Omega Instrument Ltd   69

18 Construction Industries Ltd   74

19 Baird Roofing   77

Assessing the Competition

20 Albright Ltd   81

21 Ciba-Geigy   87

22 Henshall Confectionery   90

Controlling the Marketing Function

23 Southern Steel Fabricators   95

24 Tony Sheehan 97

25 Tinsley Crouch Ltd 99

26 British United Breweries 102

Introduction

This collection of short cases is designed primarily for use in programmes and seminars where there is value in learning through discussion, yet a limit to the time available for reading and prior preparation. Each case can be read in fifteen minutes or less and discussion can start immediately after the reading.

The impact of a programme or seminar can be increased significantly with case discussion. Participation works. Perceptions of problems are heightened, and thinking patterns changed in a way that direct presentations or lectures can seldom achieve. Furthermore, the insights into problems, and the approaches and thought subroutines that are established through personal commitment to a viewpoint and developed during discussion, are retained much longer than a lecturer's generalised pearls of wisdom are remembered.

The brevity of these cases does not mean that they are easy. On the surface, many appear quite simple and the issues clear-cut. Underneath, however, the implications of any line of argument are usually extensive. Do not think that your immediate reaction is necessarily the only one. Because most cases have so many ramifications, you cannot expect to master each with one reading. Be prepared to develop and mould your thinking as the discussion progresses. On the other hand, you will gain most from a discussion session if you are big enough to take a stand early and argue why you take the stand you do.

Because the cases are so brief, many facts and details have been left out. If you consider that something left out is important, make a reasonable assumption as to what it might be in the situation described. Then argue how it would change your analysis and decision. Do not stop dead with your thinking and claim that because of some factual omission no decision can be made. You can always make decisions. More information only reduces the chance of not having made the best decision.

Actionability and precision of recommendations are important. You may feel a price increase is required, or more advertising or selling expenditure justified. If so, make up your mind exactly how you would translate your view into action. If you stop short of expressing the concrete action you have only half a prescription.

Quantification and calculation of costs, revenues and profits are equally important. Every good marketer should be able to phrase recommendations in terms of their economic consequences for costs and revenue. Remember that the difference between a successful and a failing firm is often just a small percentage of revenue. The competitive battle in many market sectors is won or lost over time from the accumulation of small differences in expenditure and small gains and losses in market share.

Finally, some cases are platforms for discussing the general issues of which they are a particular example. Your decision on the particular case will usually be a good indication of where you stand on general issues.

Consumer Motivation and the Marketing Mix

CASE 1
The Mousetrap

The following advertisement appeared on 13th April, 1977, in the *Arab Times*, an English-language newspaper published in Kuwait.

NEW SCIENTIFIC DEVICE FOR KILLING MICE

A new and advanced technology for killing mice and rats by electric sound waves.

For stores, poultry farms and other places.

NOTE: The device kills mice and rats ONLY. Tel: 447326

Kuwait's population was 950,000, of which some 450,000 were Kuwaitis and the daily circulation of the *Arab Times* was 20,000. The advertising rate in the six-page broadsheet was 4 Kuwait Dinars per cm./col. — making the cost of the advertisement 40 KD or approximately £80.00. What is your assessment of the marketing strategy adopted by the distributor?

CASE 2
Leisure Time Ice*

Richard Hendler, owner of Saxony Ice Co. in Mamaroneck, N.Y., had always been impressed when such humdrum products as water, bananas, and chicken suddenly became big sellers after they were promoted under brand names like Perrier, Chiquita, and Perdue.

Why, he wondered, couldn't the same marketing strategy work for his own product? All he had to do was come up with a brand name that the public would automatically associate with clear refreshing bags of ice.

Saxony Ice needed just such a boost. The company was founded in 1963 and, by 1975, sales were only $485,000. Hendler's customer base hadn't expanded much beyond the small set of stores that had been with him since the beginning.

Hendler realized early that a company the size of his couldn't afford to launch a widespread and effective marketing campaign singlehandedly. But there was nothing to stop him from joining forces with one or more ice companies to form a trade association, which would promote the member companies' product under a single brand name.

In 1975 Hendler and Harold Reynolds of A.T. Reynolds & Sons in Kiamesha Lake, N.Y., formed a two-man trade association under the name 'Leisure Time Ice'.

The name Leisure Time was chosen to convey the convenience of packaged ice over homemade ice. The logo — a

---

*Copyright © 1982, INC. Publishing Company, Boston, MA, USA. Reprinted with permission, *INC.*, June 1982.

snow-capped mountain backed by blue sky and surrounded by green forests — suggested a clean and refreshing product different from traditional ice packaging, which features scenes from the North Pole — igloos, Eskimos, and polar bears. Hendler and Reynolds had the logo printed on their bags, 10 trucks, and company stationery. Total cost was approximately $5,000.

At first, other ice manufacturers were sceptical of Hendler's idea to give ice new status. 'When it's hot, people buy ice', said the owners. 'In the meantime, let's continue to advertise in the *Yellow Pages*'.

But several months after the trade association was formed, another manufacturer, Richard Feingold of Bacu Ice Co., in Poughkeepsie, N.Y., began to think better of the idea and said he and some of his friends wanted to join the association.

During the next three years, Hendler, now president of Leisure Time Ice, made presentations at regional and national trade association meetings, gathering new members from Maine to Colorado. 'The more people we have, the more exposure we get, and the bigger we appear', Hendler explained to each group.

Under the association's licensing agreement, a member company used the name and logo of Leisure Time Ice and contributed advertising dollars. In all other respects, however, a member company continued to operate as a separate entity, with its own buyers, suppliers, and pricing strategy. To join the association, each company paid a membership fee based on the number of bags of ice it sold annually.

By 1978, the Leisure Time Ice Association boasted 15 members and 60 trucks. Annually, it was selling about 13 million bags of ice with the new name and logo, along with the packager's name printed discreetly at the bottom of each bag. The next step was to hire a public relations firm to tell consumers about the advantages of packaged ice. The firm chosen — Creamer, Dickson, Basford Inc. of New

York City — sent out fact sheets and news releases touting the association's message: packaged ice is taste- and odour-free and is clearer and longer-lasting than homemade ice.

The hearts of business writers and food editors from Boston to Los Angeles melted. Serious, lengthy articles were written on ice etiquette, including how many cubes to use with different drinks and how much ice to plan on per person. Hendler himself was interviewed by at least 25 editors and appeared on 15 radio and TV talk shows, holding a glass of clear, pure Leisure Time Ice cubes in one hand and a glass of cloudy, homemade cubes in the other. The *Wall Street Journal*, *New York Times*, *Los Angeles Times*, UPI, and Associated Press have all featured items on Leisure Time Ice.

Meanwhile, association members' sales increased by at least 10% a year. Hendler's own company went from $458,000 in sales in 1975 to $1,700,000 in 1981. His new business increased by 40%, and his business with existing customers expanded by 60%. 'We were the only ice manufacturers doing any advertising, and this gave us a considerable stature with buyers', Hendler says.

The association spent $50,000 for public relations in 1978, $75,000 in 1979, and $95,000 in 1980. In 1981, ads were placed in regional editions of such magazines as *Newsweek*, *Sports Illustrated*, and *Time*. One ad — a joint effort by seven members of the association — cost $24,000 to place: 'It's very impressive to walk into the office of a buyer and say, "Did you see our ad in *Newsweek*?"' remarks Hendler.

This summer the 27-member association will spend $100,000 to produce and air 30-second TV spots in areas where it has membership — the Northeast, much of the Midwest, and some of the West and Southwest. The commercial's voice-over explains why Leisure Time Ice cubes are nicer than homemade cubes. Visuals show two beverage glasses — one with cloudy cubes and one with clear cubes.

Like Perrier water, Chiquita bananas, and Perdue chickens, Leisure Time Ice may or may not have something special to offer that sets it apart from competitors. But by banding together and using their imagination, a handful of small ice manufacturers with average sales of no more than $500,000 a year have given their product something that the individual ice companies never had — national exposure and a touch of class.

CASE 3
Josiah Doncaster Ltd

On the 4th of March, the Board of Josiah Doncaster met for the second time in three weeks. The main item on the agenda, as before, was what decision to take on the proposed New Product Strategy, which arose out of the Consultant's Report commissioned by the Marketing Director.

Established in 1740, the company had built up a worldwide reputation for fine household china. Its management was paternalistic, very conservative financially, and committed to preserving company traditions. Yet over the last 10 years the company had extended its product range into industrial porcelains for high-voltage insulation, and it had been very successful.

Bill Hawkins, the newly appointed Marketing Director, opened the meeting with an aggressive presentation. At 35, he was a good 20 years younger than anyone else on the Board; and with a Harvard M.B.A., he was the only member of the Board with formal management training.

'I hope that certain members of the Board have reconsidered their positions since our last meeting. As far as I am concerned, my recommendations of three weeks ago still stand. Let's go through them once again, shall we? What are the main facts from the Consultant's Report? Let's take them one by one, shall we?

(a) At a £4.50 selling price per filter unit, and a market size of 1 million units, the present market size is £4.5 million.

(b) One company, Western Ltd, has an estimated 85% market share.

(c) The market does not like working under a monopoly, and especially as Western Ltd do not give volume discounts.

(d) The number of buying points is estimated at 20,000, of which 220 in Birmingham, 150 in London, and 70 in Manchester, take 55% of the total.

(e) There are 35 manufacturers of equipment powered by compressed air, who dominate the market; and 15 major suppliers of air compressors.

(f) Western's don't make a thing themselves — they assemble bought-in parts. So could we. There is no technical barrier to our entry into this market.

(g) Their estimated fixed costs are thought to be £100,000; with variable costs estimated at £2.7 per unit. Total cost/unit on sales of 850,000 is thought to be £2.82.

(h) Our fixed costs are estimated at £180,000; but our variable costs are clearly lower than theirs. We estimate them at £2.12 per unit. On any kind of volume the total cost of our ceramic core is down to ½p each; their sintered bronze core costs them 60p to buy in.

(i) We have a patented technological edge over Western in the ceramic core. They can only filter down to 64 microns with the sintered bronze; whereas we can tailor ours down to any desired filtration level.

(j) Finally, we have a name which is known and respected. Everyone has heard of Doncaster. We have a 200 year reputation for quality.

... So I say let's make our move. Look here ...'. He went over to the new flip chart, which was mounted on an easel, by the Adam fireplace. Pointing, he said,

> 'Page 1. Strategy: Exploit the anti-monopoly feeling of the market, our cost advantage, and our pro-

duct superiority, by launching our Filter Unit against Western.

Page 2. Tactics: Price 10% below Western. Give 25% bulk discount. Personal selling to the key buying points, and the equipment manufacturers. Sell to the rest by direct mail and trade journal advertising.

Page 3. Targets:
10% of the market in Year 1.
15% of the market in Year 2.
25% of the market in Year 3.

Page 4. Costs:

Sales in units	100,000	150,000	250,000
Fixed cost/unit	£1.80	£1.20	£0.72
Variable cost/unit	£2.12	£2.12	£2.12
Total cost	£3.92	£3.32	£2.84

Page 5. Profit/Loss:
The average price per unit is £3.48; our estimated position is

a £0.44 loss/unit year 1 i.e. £44,000 loss
a £0.16 profit/unit year 2 i.e. £ 24,000 profit
a £0.64 profit/unit year 3 i.e. £160,000 profit.

Page 6. Conclusion: The downside risks are small. Breakeven is at 13% of the market. With all we have going for us, there should be no problem in reaching breakeven, and soon!

... If we are to do our duty to the shareholders of this company, our action is clearly indicated. Our duty is clear. No further hesitation. Let's approve the project. Let's go!'

'Bill, your last remarks are totally uncalled for. This Board does not need reminding of its duty to its shareholders,' said Paul Doncaster, almost before Hawkins had sat down.

'Sorry Paul. I apologise. I guess my enthusiasm ran away with me.'

'It's my job to see that it doesn't run away with all of us. Your proposition, as you have outlined it, is too one-sided, too easy. No real account has been taken of the risks involved. And risks there are. When you have had as much experience as I have, you will realise that taking on a market leader is no easy task — especially when they are as strongly entrenched in the market as Western is in this one. 85% market share — that's market domination with a vengeance!

Filtration is their business, and they do it well. There is no complaint anywhere in the Report of their product performance, nor of their service, nor of their price. Only what amounts to a general comment that it would be nice if they were not quite so dominant! What good is that to go on? There are another 11 filter manufacturers in the market. And what have they done? Very little. They have tiny, specialised sections of the market. And their total market share adds up to what? 15% — amongst the 11 of them!

No account has been taken of Western's competitive reaction. React they will. Quickly. And hard. This isn't marginal to them as it is to us — it is their bread and butter! Market-share loss to us would hit their profits hard. The 25% market share targeted for the third year would reduce their gross profits by 25%. No company would take that quietly. We wouldn't. Why should we expect them to do so?

They have all the original equipment manufacturers sewn up; and as a result, automatically get all the replacement re-orders from the users in the factories. On average these filters last 6 years. Moreover, I doubt if any buyer regards them as a significant cost item. Take the 440 chief buyers ... in total they spend per annum about £2,475 million, i.e. £5,600 each. Since the replacement parts are bought throughout the year, this amounts to about £470 per month. This is hardly major expenditure, for the buyer of a large company.

Finally, remember that these filters are safeguards to extremely expensive machinery, and they are often specified under the terms of the guarantee. The incentives to save pennies, at the potential risk to thousands of pounds' worth of machinery is small.'

'What you say about the buyers may be right, Paul; but the Engineer is certainly aware of these filters.' Bob McGregor, a dour Scot, in his mid-sixties, and Works Director, went on, 'There is a point barely made in the Report. The life of these units averages 6 years. We find, like everyone else, that we have to clean the sintered bronze every three months. We use a caustic soda solution, then neutralise it with a weak acid. It is a costly operation, both in materials, labour, and sometimes in machine down-time. Why don't we say with our new filters, you throw away the core, and put in a new one?'

'If we did that, we'd really have to lower the price of the filter cores, and that would give the game away. The only difference between our Filter Unit and that of Western is the filter core. They even look alike, except for the difference in colour. And just because we have a price advantage, I don't see why we should charge a superior filter at a lower price in the market place. Incidentally, the Report says that the market likes the clear plastic bowl, because they can see the residue left by the filter. But I remember, and my staff have looked it up, that there was a court case in 1962, when one of these plastic bowls exploded, after an air pressure surge down the pipe line. There was a lot of publicity at the time. Very unfavourable. Don't let me lose sight of the fact that 80% of this company's profits, almost £1.74 million, come from the household china division. Anything that might put that at risk needs to be looked at very closely. If we go into this field at all, then we can't risk the use of a plastic bowl. We must use something stronger, a metal, or a metal alloy.' John Davies, the longest serving member of the Board, and the Financial Director, finished speaking abruptly, when he saw that Hawkins had risen to his feet to make a reply.

'But to do that, John, would be to go against what the market demands. You must give the market what it wants.'

'No Bill, we don't have to in this particular case,' said Paul Doncaster. 'I'm not altogether happy with the proposal as it stands, and I think that other members of the Board feel the same. Perhaps we would be well advised to commission a more general survey into potential new products, which don't involve a risk to our main product line, and don't involve taking on a dominant market leader.

I propose, notwithstanding your enthusiasm, Bill, that we take no further action on this Report, and commission a more general survey into the possibility of product diversification. I formally propose this to the Board. May I have your votes please?'

Market Measurement and Research

CASE 4
Ampex Videocassette Tapes

Early in 1985, Edwin Pessara, magnetic tape marketing director for Ampex Corporation, was considering whether to recommend that Ampex re-enter the United States consumer market for blank videocassette tapes. The USA was a nation of avid TV viewers. Its 85 million homes averaged over 40 hours' viewing per week. Ampex had taken an earlier decision to opt out of the consumer sector because of cutthroat price competition. The take-off in consumer tape demand over the past two years, however, had been extremely rapid and Pessara felt that prices would now stabilise. Furthermore, if Ampex did not take this opportunity to establish its brand at the basic consumer level, he felt that those who did would threaten Ampex's long-established position in sales of videotape for professional uses and even its magnetic computer tape sales. Ampex had no spare production capacity so it would have to buy in tape or invest in a new plant.

Sales of blank cassettes had jumped to about 100 million units in 1984 from 63 million the year before and 25 million in 1982. The trade press predicted over 120 million in 1985. Behind this growth in demand lay a significant increase in the recording of TV programmes for later viewing. Viewers were using their videocassette recorders (VCRs) much more for this purpose than to view prerecorded tapes which sold only 10 million in 1983 and 20 million in 1984. For every such sale, however, there were about 10 rentals of prerecorded tapes. Sales of new VCRs had also increased to 7.6 million units in 1984 and the forecast was for 9 million in 1985. These figures represented a large increase on the 4.2

million units sold in 1983, which itself had doubled the total number of VCRs in use in the USA.

The blank tape industry had become locked in a fierce price war started by 3M's Scotch brand. The average wholesale price of a blank tape had dropped from $11.34 in 1982 to $6.58 in 1984 and was forecast at $6.14 for 1985. Richard G. Mueller, 3M's marketing operations manager for magnetic products, was quoted as saying, 'We all see this big carrot and we're all going after it'. He had relentlessly courted retailers for shelf space, and he had introduced a cash rebate on blank tapes. 'Rebates means the consumer gets the discount but the retailer still makes money', Mueller explained. When competitors followed 3M, Mueller had countered with rebates plus gifts, such as a round-trip ticket on any Republic Airlines' flight, for buying 20 of 3M's $10 tapes, or free dinners at Victoria Station restaurants.

John Hollands, President of Sony Tape Sales Co., told reporters: '3M's corporate policy over the past year has been to buy market share at any cost. We felt we had to match their best offer, so it ends up costing us both money'. Hollands thought the first firms to drop out would be those that packaged and marketed tape bought in bulk from the six major manufacturers who sold to others as well as marketing their own brands: Sony, TDK, 3M (Scotch), Hitachi (Maxell), Tandy (Memorex) or Fuji. These six firms produced over 80% of all videotape sold in the United States and supplied over sixty other firms.

Those who did not manufacture, however, disagreed that they would be forced out. They pointed to the keen competition between these six manufacturers as well as the possibility of overseas supply. Both Kodak and Polaroid bought in tape and felt that their strong brand identification with consumers would enable them to command a continued price premium. The general manager of marketing in Kodak's consumer electronic division agreed that outside sourcing put pressure on margins but argued that, as they had no significant capital investment in the business, the margin they required was much lower.

TDK supplied Kodak and had led the market before 3M's move. Their director of sales and marketing felt that the worst of the price war was over and that prices would stabilise at $5 or $6 for a standard-grade tape. 'Right now demand is increasing', he said, 'but nobody is building new facilities. Since a new tape plant is very expensive we are approaching the point where this industry reaches capacity'.

A new tape plant cost around $120 million with a capacity of possibly 20 million tapes per annum. Manufacturing and packaging, allowing for 10% depreciation, cost around $3 per unit, with distribution, promotion and retail markups adding at least $1.50 per unit. On the revenue side, blank tapes in the 120-minute length ran from $37 for 3M's top-of-the-line 'HGX Plus' tape all the way down to $4, after discounting and rebates, for standard-grade cassettes. Promotion of higher-grade tapes to build margins, however, was of only limited success. Consumers seemed to have caught on to the fact that there was not much difference technically between $5 tapes and $20 tapes. Over 85% of tape sales were accounted for by standard grades.

There were some really cheap tapes as low as $3 on super-special offers. If substandard, however, these could gum up a VCR's recording heads. There was also a possibility that more very cheap tapes might be introduced by the Koreans and Taiwanese to accompany very inexpensive VCR machines which they were poised to introduce.

CASE 5
Chez Nouveau Furnishings

William Elliot, store manager for Chez Nouveau, was considering whether to submit a proposal to the Board for a major reallocation of floor space to customer services. Chez Nouveau was located in one of London's main shopping streets and its four floors were primarily devoted to household furnishing departments.

Six months previously, a two-week comparison of the daily traffic through the store and the daily number of purchases suggested that at least 77% of those entering the store made no purchases at all. In an effort to raise the percentage who bought in the store, Elliot had increased the frequency of manufacturers' demonstrations and special offers. These efforts had produced results. Electronic counters installed at both store entrances showed that over the past two months daily average store traffic had increased 3% to 2,330 and average daily purchases to 618.

The aim of the new proposals was to go one step further and increase both the percentage of customers actually buying and the average amount spent, through lengthening the time spent in the store. The entire top floor would be rearranged to provide a customer restaurant for light snacks and luncheons and an art gallery. There would be a reduction of 6% in the floor space devoted to Chez Nouveau merchandise, but Elliot estimated that he would be able to recoup two-thirds of the normal net revenue from the franchisees of the services.

Elliot's proposals stemmed from a second consultant study that had stationed researchers at both store entrances for two days to query a random sample of entrants about their purchase intentions. Those interviewed were invited to check back on leaving the store for a free canvas shopping bag. At that point, they were asked further questions about what they had bought in the store. Nearly 90% returned for the second set of questions, and the following summary of research was tabulated:

Intention to Buy No. of Items	No. of Replies	\multicolumn{6}{c}{Actual Purchases}					
		0	1	2	3	4	5
0	153	120	19	6	4	2	2
1	263	210	32	7	7	4	3
2	164	109	26	15	7	5	2
3	62	39	8	6	6	2	1
4	20	8	5	2	3	2	—
5	5	2	2	—	1	—	—
	667	488	92	36	28	15	8

Time Spent in Store	0	1	2	3	4	5
Under 20 mins	174	30	5	6	1	—
20–39	163	35	13	10	3	2
40–59	74	12	11	6	4	3
60–79	39	5	4	5	3	2
80–99	31	8	1	1	2	1
100 & over	7	2	2	—	2	—
	488	92	36	28	15	8

CASE 6
Dornbusch Corporation

On completion of his B.A. in marketing through the sandwich course at Midland Polytechnic, Graham Stoddard was particularly pleased when he was recruited as UK product manager (electric razors) for the Dornbusch Corporation. Dornbusch had a world-wide name in the consumer electrical products field and its brands had been aggressively promoted for many years. The firm had a reputation as a leader in marketing practice and as an excellent training ground for senior marketing posts later in an executive's career.

To Graham's growing astonishment when he started his new job, he could find from internal Dornbusch records no hard data about what was happening in the user market for electric razors and very little on the outlet market. Large retail chains had been demanding and obtaining special deals and it was not clear where, and even at what price, Dornbusch razors were being sold. Promotion costs were running at 20% of revenue, but there appeared to be a very low correlation between promotion and sales patterns over the years.

Dornbusch's current sales were around 210,000 razors per annum — all aimed at the male market. Estimates from the IPC Marketing Manual put the UK market two years previously at 1.6 million units, of which around 10% were probably women's shavers. Dornbusch's estimated 15% of the men's segment placed them well behind Philips with an estimated 800,000 units and Braun with possibly 400,000.

Stoddard knew he could obtain more precise estimates of current sales from A.C. Nielsen surveys of outlets, but he decided that it was more important to find out where the future potential really lay. There had been years of expanding demand and much switching and upgrading by users. Was the future potential in first purchase, replacement or second use? Or was there little potential left at all? Of 20 million male shavers it had been estimated that 70% were still wet shavers. After a little questioning around, Graham was fairly certain that he would get immediate clearance for a research commitment of up to £10,000. On such a budget he estimated he could finance a survey of 2,000 adult males, provided he arranged for the analysis of the results internally and kept the data requested fairly short. He accordingly drew up the following five open-ended questions to be asked of 2,000 randomly selected males aged between 20 and 55:

> What type of razor do you now own?
> How long have you had it?
> What type of razor did you have before this one?
> Have you ever owned any other kind?
> When did you switch and why?

Graham hoped that, armed with this information, he could pull more through from internal sales records and fairly firmly establish the need for an ongoing feedback system.

Audit Answers Ltd had been recommended to Graham as young, keen and hungry. His approach to them confirmed that they were what he was looking for. They were well prepared to carry through the national survey for £10,000 and turn over the interview sheets to Dornbusch for analysis.

Determining Product Features

CASE 7
Waste Water

Having read that pure human waste water was fetching up to £30 per cup in the United States, Victor Moon had decided to set up a business in the United Kingdom. Enquiries showed that he would be able without much difficulty to obtain and regularly check supplies from carefully vetted individuals. He knew that the market would be much smaller than that in the US and he was now concerned with how to identify purchasers and reach them.

As far as Victor could ascertain, the US market came mainly from among the 2 million who were asked in any year by employers or potential employers to submit to urine tests for drug screening. Addicts were buying pure human waste water contained in small balloons in a range of flesh colours which they taped to their inner thigh. They then squeezed the balloon at the appropriate moment to produce what appeared to be their own sample. They apparently could easily deceive any doctor or nurse who was present to ensure that the jar was not filled from a pocketed container.

Questions

(a) Is it acceptable to market this product?
(b) Is participation in any aspect of marketing this product simply a matter for personal decision or should there be legislation against it?
(c) What exactly is the basis on which you determine acceptability or unacceptability?

(d) Do you have the same view about all other products that exhibit similar characteristics? If not, state how you differentiate.
(e) If waste water were to be successfully marketed, what channel of distribution would be most appropriate?
(f) Describe the advertising or promotion that might be appropriate.
(g) How should the product be priced?

CASE 8
Graham's Groceries Ltd

The supermarket chain invasion was beginning to bite in the late 1950s when George Graham took over the family grocery store in one of those exclusive little towns just past the Greater London green belt. George had nevertheless done remarkably well in the face of this cut-price, fish-finger invasion. As tenants' leases fell due, he had been able to expand to take the entire floor space of Graham's High Street building. This had given 500 square metres of floor space and George was able to move early into self-service, while retaining counter service for fresh meat and fresh fruit and vegetables and even a little flower shop and coffee shop. Wherever possible, he included some high-priced and exclusive brand items in Graham's range. These items had a slower turnover, but the higher margins compensated somewhat and kept Graham's image above that of the standard supermarket.

By 1973 frozen foods were becoming increasingly popular and George decided to expand his range to include numerous gourmet items. He knew that many of his customers still did not own freezers, so to develop their custom he launched a 'Gourmet Club'. He set up a display in the centre of the store with a 16 cubic feet deep freezer as the centrepiece. Customers who signed up as Gourmet Club members could purchase the freezer at a price below the best discount house prices and pay the purchase price of £20.00 per month. To join the Club, customers signed an agreement to purchase a minimum of £20.00 per month of frozen foods from the Gourmet Club list at prices £5 below Graham's normal retail price. Purchases were recorded against a Club charge number and the customer billed the previous month's outstanding balance. The Club idea caught on rapidly and within six months had 100 members.

Many times Mr Graham was asked by potential Club members whether he would extend the scheme to refrigerators and freezer-refrigerators. This gave George the idea of adding a line of appliances and electrical goods to Graham's range. He could use one of the front corners of the store facing the High Street and extend the display right into the window. For appliances, wholesale prices were 50% below suggested retail prices. This would give a chance for special promotions, while still leaving substantially higher gross margins than Graham's store average of 19% on sales.

CASE 9
Ansafone Corporation

In April 1982, Frank Rogers, non-executive chairman of Ansafone Corporation, was concerned about how the company could exploit the recently-liberalised UK market for telephone answering machines (TAMs) and reverse its loss of £900,000 for the year to 31st March 1982. Ansafone's

Exhibit 1 *Ansafone Telephone Answering Machines, April 1982*

Model	Features	Annual Rent £	New Rentals (Units) 1981–2 (actual)	1982–3 (budgeted)
6	Answering and recording, dual tape.	180	1,800	—
6A	As 6, plus choice of only answering.	230	1,050	4,700
600	As 6A, *plus* will not answer if cassette full, 2-way recording, remote playback to voice or bleeper coding, dictation facility.	290	1,400	1,160
7	Voice-controlled recording; 2-hour capacity. 2-way recording, dictation, dual tape.	300	90	100
7P	As 7, plus voice-coded playback.	240	1,000	1,400
S100	Simple play and answer, dual tape.	110	570	1,400
			5,910	8,760

main business was the leasing of TAMs. Their models ranged from simple dual tape machines to those with sophisticated remote control and extended recording capacity (Exhibit 1).

Connection to the public network of user-owned, rather than leased, TAMs had been permitted by British Telecom as from 1st October 1981. For the first three years this permission would be extended only to a small range of British-made products. Nevertheless, the difficulty of selling TAM rentals was already increasing.

Ansafone's Sales Manager, Mr Clarke, was concerned at the recent increase in salesperson turnover, resulting in his opinion from 'loss of confidence'. The 1981—2 turnover was around 75% against the normal level of around 50% per year. Quotas had been set on the basis of new annual rental per salesperson of £31,000, to cover costs and give a reasonable profit. In 1981—2, however, only 9 out of 110 sales staff reached this target. Mr Clarke had accordingly raised the minimum standard from £18,000 to £24,000 retaining the target of £31,000. He also instituted a 'quota club' with an annual prize for those who reached 100%. Statistics on sales operations are shown in Exhibit 2.

New Rentals

About 50% of new rentals came from enquiries, the rest from direct approach, starting with 'cold' telephone calls. The historical conversion of enquiries to sales had been about 40%, but had been dropping. Exhibit 3 shows a recent analysis of a sample of enquiries. Enquiries themselves had also been dropping. The publicity budget had therefore been increased from £300,000 for 1982—3, with half earmarked for advertising, £100,000 for promotion, and the rest for miscellaneous costs. Last year, Ansafone had spent £50,000 on Yellow Pages advertising and £30,000 on local classified ads. Staff could see very little pattern to customers, and found it impossible to predict from 9 million

Exhibit 2 *Sales Statistics*

Average TAM Salesperson Weekly Performance

Direct Approach Calls	60.0
Demonstrations	6.6
Contracts	1.1
Enquiries	3.4
Demonstrations	2.0
Contracts	1.0

Forms of Commission

(1) No salary, £4,500 advance on commission
    37% commission on first year's rental
(2) Basic £4,000, £2,000 advance on commission
    19% commission on first year's rental

Sales Cost per Contract 1981–2
Budget — £220
Actual — £270

Exhibit 3 *Sales Enquiry Analysis, March 1982*

	Enquiries	Contracts	Conversion (%)
Local Classified Ads	75	30	40
Users	60	40	67
British Telecom	20	5	25
Yellow Pages	300	75	25
Reputation	250	50	20
Recommendation	30	15	50
Total	735	215	29

business telephone lines which few would rent a TAM. Consequently there was no segment targeting of advertising, and cold calling took in all businesses in the area.

Contract Renewals/Cancellations

Mr Clarke was also concerned about the rising level of cancellations of contracts. In 1981–2, Ansafone gained nearly 6,000 contracts and lost over 8,000. A feature of the rental contract was that it automatically renewed, and six months' advance written notice was required for cancellation even at the *end* of the typical 3-year contract. An analysis had shown that cancellations fell roughly into the following categories:

	1981–2
Bad debts/gone out of business	2,200
Closing down	1,000
No further need	2,000
Going for purchase substitute	3,000
	8,200

Executives argued that only the 'bottom end' of the customer base, the smallest and most financially insecure, was being lost, either by substitution to purchased machines or by insolvency because of the recession. Moreover, the impact on the rental income was still only marginal. Ansafone's revenue was £11.2 million for 1981–2, although it had to bear a write-off of £1 million on new products that had not caught on. In addition, the 'rental base' of rents up to renewal dates for the 48,000 outstanding contracts at 31st December 1981 totalled £21.2 million. This was a definite asset, although it did not show on Ansafone's balance sheet (Exhibit 4).

In taking steps to halt the erosion, Mr Clarke had arranged in March for Rentals Administration to inform Sales of impending cancellations by forwarding the written notices received. Discounts of up to 35% on rental renewals were now authorised to be proffered, in stages, by the salesforce. Commission would be paid to sales staff as if the full annual rental had been obtained.

Exhibit 4 *Ansafone Corporation Balance Sheet as at 31st March 1982 (£ millions)*

Funds Employed	
Share Capital and Reserves	6.5
Long-term Loans	2.2
	8.7
Represented by	
Land, Buildings, Fixtures, Plant & Vehicles (Estimated Current Market Value £2.7 m.)	2.3
Equipment on Hire (ECMV £8.0 m.)	11.0
Total Fixed Assets	13.3
Stock and Work in Progress	3.1
Debtors	2.1
Current Assets	5.2
Creditors	(2.0)
Bank Overdraft (Limit £9 m.)	(7.8)
Current Liabilities	(9.8)
Deficit on Working Capital	(4.6)
Net Assets	8.7

Competition

Despite spending some £300,000 annually on research and development, Ansafone had found no answer to the growing sales inroads of pirate companies. Before liberalisation, small importers had been selling TAMs illegally in the UK. Now *sale* was legal, although *use* on the public network remained technically illegal. Answercall, which entered the market in 1979 as an 'illegal pirate' selling unlicensed machines from the Far East, was the most successful. It had sold around 90,000 unlicensed machines and expected to continue at an equivalent annual rate of 30,000. Its advertising claimed: 'A large number of companies automatically renew their rental contracts because they have a trouble-free machine without realising that they can drastically reduce costs by buying instead'. However, at least one small importer had gone into liquidation in 1981 because its sales volume did not generate enough margin to cover heavy promotional costs.

The heavy advertising and low purchase prices of the pirates (Exhibit 5), compared with Ansafone's rental-only rates and prices of the few other licensed manufacturers, had stimulated the market to an annual value of approximately £50 million. New methods of distribution had also fuelled the growth, including mail-order advertisements in *Exchange and Mart* and a growing number of small local retail outlets, many set up by ex-TAM-rental sales staff.

Exhibit 5   *Retail Prices of Competing TAMs*

	Light Usage	Heavy Usage
Non-Remote Control	£65–£100	£100–£160
Remote Control	£100–£150	£170 upwards

Service, Rental, and Production Operations

As against the competition, the Chairman could see a major strength in Ansafone's service and rental administration. The nationwide service organisation employed 157 staff and offered same-day service or replacement. This service cost Ansafone £29 per installed machine in 1981–2, but was considered essential for businesses relying on TAMs. In comparison, competitors selling through distributors offered only a one-year warranty, then an annual maintenance contract at £30 per annum. Moreover, the customer had to send in the machine for service or repair and would be without a TAM during that period. Competitors claimed, though, that only 2% of machines were expected to give trouble once in a useful life of 5 to 6 years. Ansafone's rental administration employed a staff of 70 costing about half as much as the service organisation, and was also regarded as extremely well organised and administered. Both service and rental units were 'capable of absorbing new products, more contracts, and new conditions of business, such as hire purchase'.

Manufacture of new products was also an alternative. Ansafone manufactured all TAM equipment from basic components, buying in tape transport mechanisms from a large UK manufacturer. Manufacturing staff were now down to 40, one-fifth the number of two years earlier. As most were engaged in refurbishing used rental machines, there were few economies of scale in new manufacture. New Ansafone TAMs cost on average £200 in direct labour and materials. The solid design of the models that had previously been specified by British Telecom made it hard to reduce these costs. There was also about £800,000 of factory overheads currently arising. But the facilities were modern and bright and capable of carrying four or five times the output.

Distribution

CASE 10
Chalfont Bedspreads

John Blore, the new Commercial Manager of Chalfont Bedspreads Ltd of Manchester, had concluded that the best way to increase Chalfont's static sales of patterned cotton bedspreads was to extend sales coverage to large retail furniture stores. Blore's investigation of the United Kingdom market figures had disclosed that more than twice as many mattresses were sold annually as bedspreads. Blore was certain that many people did not use bedspreads and that there was an unfilled demand that could be reached by selling bedspreads at the time people were buying bedroom furniture. Already a few furniture firms were selling household textiles, including sheets, blankets, duvets and bedspreads; moreover, retail furniture salesmen were generally paid an incentive commission of around 2% and bedspread sales would add to their earnings.

All Chalfont's £3 million sales were made through the Crane Sales Agency whose 15 salesmen called on some 450 wholesalers, multiples and large department stores, representing the lines of a number of textile manufacturers. Crane received a normal commission of 5% on Chalfont turnover, but Blore realised that some incentive would be needed to compensate for the cost of breaking into the new outlets. He was prepared to increase the commission to 7½% for the first year's orders from new outlets. Some of the increase would presumably be paid as an additional incentive to the Crane salesforce who received a straight 2% commission on sales, yet the remainder would make a significant contribution to Crane's profit. Chalfont already represented 25% of Crane's turnover.

Blore was also contemplating a television campaign. Chalfont bedspreads presented a very colourful range that, allowing for retail store margins of around 30% on sales, retailed from £14 to £36 each. He could envisage a kaleidoscope of colour in short spot advertising on national TV. Competing mattress firms regularly advertised their brands, but to date no bedspread firm had mounted a campaign.

CASE 11
Integrated Offices Ltd

Integrated Offices Ltd manufactured and sold worldwide a wide line of computers, terminals, printers, copiers and ancillary equipment for offices. Staff were regularly reminded from the centre that the firm's mission lay in providing 'The Office of the Future'. With this in mind, the extensive national television campaign run by the firm's UK subsidiary conveyed the message that IOL could equip an office that would automate all office functions with great savings in labour cost and more rapid production of all its output.

The firm sold its range primarily through office equipment dealers who held exclusive rights within a defined territory around their base location. IOL's representatives spent much of their time advising these dealers on how to target customers, plot their sales approach, arrange for installation and provide after-sales service. IOL representatives were also used extensively by dealers as technical advisers. They were required, therefore, to have considerable knowledge of office procedures and systems as well as technical skill and knowledge of the product line.

The company had always found it difficult to get dealer staff to do a really professional job representing the IOL line. Many dealers wanted to be little more than passive order takers and most staff did not have the product or system knowledge and experience to do the job well. Most tended to sell equipment by item rather than by system and to minimise their pre- and post-sale effort. Over the past year or two, IOL sales management felt that there had been a marked decrease in quality and effort among dealer staff.

In response to the dealership problem, IOL's Managing Director had decided to set up a chain of company-owned outlets in major metropolitan areas. He believed that performance of higher quality sales staff would easily justify the considerable investment in leases, inventory and working capital. IOL's Marketing Director, however, was sceptical. Even using all his existing representatives, he did not have sufficient staff of the right calibre to man the new outlets.

CASE 12
Metropolitan National Bank Ltd

As Chief Properties Manager for the Metropolitan, Brent Elliott held overall responsibility for negotiating purchases of new sites, construction of new premises, and disposal of properties no longer required by the bank. Metropolitan operated over 1,000 branches in the United Kingdom; consequently Brent was concerned with numerous building and renovation projects at any one time.

Brent was annoyed. His professional competence had been indirectly criticised during a recent regional management meeting when the Properties Division was blamed for failing to provide adequate teller windows and floor area for waiting customers in a branch opened only six months previously. Design and construction of this particular branch had extended over four years and there had been more new office buildings in the immediate vicinity than expected when the designs were drawn up. Moreover, no competitor banks had moved in to take up the additional growth. Anyway, Brent was sure the design would have been adequate, had it not been for the large numbers of customers using the branch facilities whose accounts were with other Metropolitan branches or other banks entirely.

Customers of any Metropolitan branch could use their cash cards to obtain cash from the new branch's cash dispensing machines — two inside and one outside. Alternatively they, along with anyone else, could withdraw up to £50 in cash from the four tellers' windows by presenting their cheque card with their cheque. These facilities had encouraged customers to leave their accounts with their original branches and to use the new branch as a convenient cash point. At peak times, the lines at the tellers' windows were becoming entangled with the lines for the cash dispensers on the opposite wall. There was no reserve floor space in the branch, however, and it would be difficult to add even one more dispenser.

It seemed to Brent that heavy traffic through the new branch was an indication of success in choosing a good site, not a cause for criticism. Still, he planned to avoid criticism in future by asking a consulting firm to develop a standard procedure for forecasting customer traffic for any potential branch location. Before he did so, however, Brent thought he should make a preliminary list of the considerations that the consultants should allow for in their procedure.

CASE 13
Aigle Engineering

Aigle Engineering Ltd was a precision engineering shop of 35 employees in south Manchester managed by the 51-year-old owner, Alan Mohr. Mohr had started the business ten years previously, taking on jobbing work that other firms priced to avoid. He had, however, kept a continual lookout for specialised products that would give him a stable work load. Three years ago, after manufacturing several batches of hand presses for pressing simple metal pin badges, Alan had acquired the rights to the press from its designer. The firm selling the blanks, rings and pins for the badges were happy for Aigle to take over the direct supply and warranty for the presses. They referred all enquiries to him, often stimulated by their own advertising, and a steady volume of orders came in from around the world. A press cost about £500, and the typical order came from a novelty store owner, a small entrepreneur who sold badges at fairs and shows or someone who circulated clubs or political parties offering to produce an appropriate badge for them.

Before he set up Aigle Engineering, Alan Mohr had been works engineer for a sewing machine manufacturer, and for many years he had pursued a hobby of adapting sewing machines to new or extended uses. Eight months ago, he had finally perfected an electronically-guided, multi-headed machine for high-speed sewing of shirt collars. Thinking he would get many enquiries from shirt manufacturers, Alan had shown the machine, for which he had applied for a patent, on a small stand at this year's Textile Machinery Exhibition in Munich. A reporter from a machinery journal was attending the show and had included

Exhibit 1 *Moreno Equipment Inc., Manufacturers of Textile Machinery & Equipment*

Aigle Engineering Ltd,
64 Penine Drive,
Sale,
Cheshire,
United Kingdom.

Attention: Mr Alan Mohr

Dear Mr Mohr

On his return from Munich, Mr William Shergold commented favourably on your Aigle Multi-Collar machine. Mr Shergold was unable to see the machine on other than a short test operation but we understand that you have several prototypes that are being tested by local manufacturers. We are wondering, therefore, if you would consider freighting us one of these when current tests are completed so that we might assess its potential in various applications.

In the meantime, we would be very pleased to know what you would propose regarding a license for manufacturing by ourselves. As we believe that the market for the machine would be limited, we suggest that you might be prepared to consider granting us world manufacturing rights. Alternatively, we would consider world rights excluding the European Community.

We await your reply with interest.

Sincerely yours,

Klaus Graham
Manager, Licensor Relations

---

a piece on Aigle's machine in the journal's 'What's New' section.

As a result of this exposure, Alan had received two letters from firms wishing to distribute his machine — one from New Jersey, USA, and the other from Korea. The Korean firm, Soon Lee & Co., was an importer in Seoul and was asking for permission to import and sell within the Korean market. The New Jersey firm, Moreno Equipment Inc., on the other hand, manufactured a range of machinery and was interested in manufacturing rights. One of its executives had visited Aigle's stand in Munich and spent a lot of time examining the prototype. His letter is reproduced in Exhibit 1.

Alan was tempted to give Moreno the world manufacturing rights because his existing staff were not really experienced in electronic work. The additional working capital required would also be high for a firm that had strained to capitalise itself out of the profits he had not withdrawn. Of the three prototypes, each so far had cost about £20,000 in materials and manufacturing time. Mohr wondered what terms he should offer Moreno and whether he should airfreight one of the prototypes to New Jersey.

Promotion

CASE 14
Agency 5

Agency 5 prided itself on its global capability. The advantage of an internationally-coordinated promotional strategy was highlighted in the agency's own promotional literature and it had recently sponsored a series of papers on global marketing and distributed them worldwide.

One of Agency 5's prime accounts was Consumer Electrical, for whom they handled advertising in over thirty countries. Peter Orpington, Agency 5's director for the Consumer Electrical account in London, had recently been asked to a briefing by the UK management of Consumer's television division. The briefing called for a significant repositioning of Consumer's television line in the United Kingdom. With some cosmetic upgrading to the models, the line was to be given a new upmarket quality image, priced at a premium, and sold in substantially reduced volumes.

This repositioning was a reaction to international competitors who had turned the UK into a major battleground over the previous two years. Competitors' determined efforts to gain UK market share seemed to be based on a belief that UK success was the key to further penetration elsewhere. Margins in the UK had fallen drastically as a result.

Consumer's UK television division and the management of the UK national subsidiary to whom it reported were, however, largely measured by profit achievement. Their new repositioning, while a strategic retreat, would at least maintain a profit on the reduced UK sales for a few years. On the other hand, the image would be at marked variance with that elsewhere. Peter Orpington had the overall positioning brief from the Agency 5 office serving Consumer Electrical's central unit responsible for television strategy. It clearly placed the line as reasonably priced and a volume seller.

Orpington wondered whether he should take some steps to persuade the UK television management to reconcile its move with Consumer Electrical's advertising brief. He thought perhaps, if he sent copies of the proposals that he was preparing to the Agency 5 unit serving Consumer's head office, that might also produce some reaction.

CASE 15
A Line from Sally

Sally did not like the advertisement she had just seen in the office copy of *Forbes*. It showed a bikini-clad surf skier with the bold heading: **THIS LADY IS BEING PULLED BY HER VOLVO**. It did not even show the boat — only the nearly waist-high towing rope leading to it. Sally guessed, however, that a complaint would be useless. Last time she had complained about an advertisement she had come off second-best in the correspondence. To get anywhere, she would have to argue that the ad was likely to cause 'grave or widespread offence'. It was offensive to her, but was that enough?

On the earlier occasion, Sally had written directly to the Managing Director of the Sally Line after she had received some good-natured ribbing from two male acquaintances. On the train coming up to London in the morning they had pointed out an advertisement in the *Daily Mail* that claimed in big letters: ONLY SALLY WILL GO ALL THE WAY FOR £58 (Exhibit 1). On arriving at the office, Sally wrote as follows:

> I should like to register a very strong complaint about the advertising approach used by the Sally Line in its recent newspaper campaign. Your bold headline 'ONLY SALLY WILL GO ALL THE WAY FOR £58' is definitely in poor taste.
>
> As somebody named Sally long before your line, I feel that I should speak up on behalf of all the other Sally's of this world who have received the numerous ribald comments from those seeing your ads. Readership of the newspapers in which you have placed your ad is very high indeed and it is very likely that there are several hundred thousand Sally's who feel

Exhibit 1 *Advertisement in the 'Daily Mail', Saturday 4th June, 1983*

> # ONLY SALLY WILL GO ALL THE WAY FOR £58.
>
> Our daytime, summer family fares are the lowest you'll find across the Channel. Check them for yourself. You'll be glad you did.
>
> | | |
> |---|---|
> | P&O Ferries DOVER–BOULOGNE | £79 |
> | Townsend Thoresen DOVER–CALAIS | £79 |
> | Sealink DOVER–DUNKIRK | £67·50 |
> | SALLY LINE RAMSGATE–DUNKIRK | £58 |
>
> PRICES FOR SINGLE FARE, SAILING BETWEEN 10AM AND 5PM JULY–AUG. 1983: 2 ADULTS, 2 CHILDREN (UNDER 14), CAR LENGTH 4.0–4.5 METRES.
>
> Write or 'phone for our 1983 brochure, Sally Line Ltd., Ramsgate Harbour, Kent CT11 8RP. (0843 55522). Or London 01-409 2240, Birmingham 021-236 4010, Manchester 061-228 0040.
>
> Name_____
> Address_____
>
> DA 4/6

aggrieved at your advertisement. The sexist innuendos, moreover, are the sort of thing the advertising agency should have advised you against.

Can you please assure me that this campaign will be terminated immediately?

Yours faithfully,

Sally Rimes

Back came the following reply from the Sally Line Marketing Manager:

Dear Ms. Rimes,

I must say that we are totally amazed by your letter in that our headline should ever be thought to be in anything but excellent taste, as it simply made the statement that Sally would go all the way for £58 and this purely meant what it said; we as Sally Line, for that is our name, would carry a cross-Channel passenger and his car for a total of £58.00. Any other obtuse meaning had never entered our head.

I note you state that you held the name Sally long before our Line. I would point out that Sally Viking Line has, in fact, been in existence in the Baltic for a total of 38 years and, of course, I cannot draw any comparisons personally.

I must say that you have been the first Sally in the world to take objection to us using the name of our own Company in any advertising and I am most perturbed that you would have the type of friend that would make ribald comments to you concerning a ferry company's advertising as this would seem totally irrelevant.

In view of the above, I can only assure you that it is our intention to continue with our advertising campaign as it exists.

Yours sincerely,

John G. Kilroy
Marketing Manager

This reply showed even less taste than the advertisement, so Sally lodged an official complaint with the Advertising Standards Authority. The ASA was founded as a 'self-regulatory' body to promote and enforce 'the highest standards of advertising in all media'. In practice, however, because it was funded by a surcharge on gross billings apart from radio and television, policing of those two media was left to the Independent Broadcasting Authority. Mail-order catalogues and advertising aimed at foreign audiences were also excluded. The chairman of the ASA Council was appointed from outside the advertising business and in turn appointed the Council members — a majority of whom had also to be from outside advertising. The Council adjudicated on all consumer complaints according to the British Code of

Exhibit 2 *British Code of Advertising Practice: General Rules*

	All advertisements should be legal, decent, honest and truthful
Legality	1.1 Advertisements should contain nothing which is in breach of the law, nor omit anything which the law requires.
	1.2 Advertisements should not encourage or condone defiance of the law.
Decency	2 Advertisements should contain nothing which is likely, in the light of generally prevailing standards of decency and propriety, to cause grave or widespread offence.
	2.1 The purpose of the Code is to control the content of advertisements, not to hamper the sale of products which may be found offensive, for whatever reason, by some people. Provided, therefore, that advertisements for such products are not themselves offensive, there will normally be no ground for objection to them in terms of this section of the Code (Cf. II 4.2.2 and 4.2.6).
Honesty	3 Advertisements should not be so framed as to abuse the trust of consumers or exploit their lack of experience or knowledge.
Truthful presentation	4.1 All descriptions, claims and comparisons which relate to matters of objectively ascertainable fact should be capable of substantiation. **Advertisers and advertising agencies are required to hold such substantiation ready for production immediately to the CAP Committee or the Advertising Standards Authority.** They should compile a statement outlining substantiation and have it available *before* offering an advertisement for publication.
	4.2 **Advertisements should not contain statements or visual presentations which,**

> directly or by implication, by omission, ambiguity, or exaggeration, are likely to mislead the consumer about the product advertised, the advertiser, or about any other product or advertiser.

Advertising Practice which is set out in Exhibit 2. This code was drafted and amended by the ASA Code of Advertising Practice Committee made up of some 20 representatives from advertisers, agencies and media. Although the Code was subject to approval by the ASA Council, in practice it was within the control of the advertising industry.

Sally's complaint went through the ASA Complaints Procedure (Exhibit 3) and was rejected by the Council. The complaint rejection letter stated:

> In our view, and on the facts available to us, there does not seem to be a prima facie case for investigation here, since the advertisement is unlikely to cause grave or widespread offence and is not, therefore, in breach of Section III, 2. of the British Code of Advertising Practice.

Exhibit 3 *Summary of ASA Complaints Procedure*

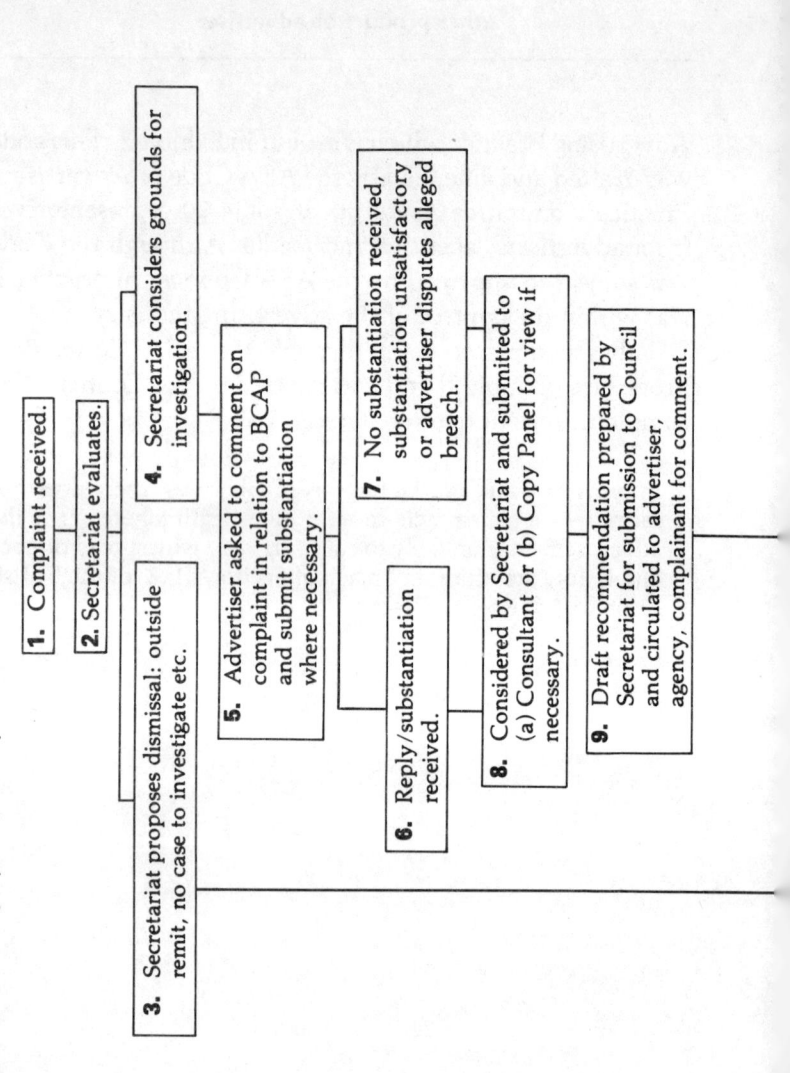

1. Complaint received.
2. Secretariat evaluates.
3. Secretariat proposes dismissal: outside remit, no case to investigate etc.
4. Secretariat considers grounds for investigation.
5. Advertiser asked to comment on complaint in relation to BCAP and submit substantiation where necessary.
6. Reply/substantiation received.
7. No substantiation received, substantiation unsatisfactory or advertiser disputes alleged breach.
8. Considered by Secretariat and submitted to (a) Consultant or (b) Copy Panel for view if necessary.
9. Draft recommendation prepared by Secretariat for submission to Council and circulated to advertiser, agency, complainant for comment.

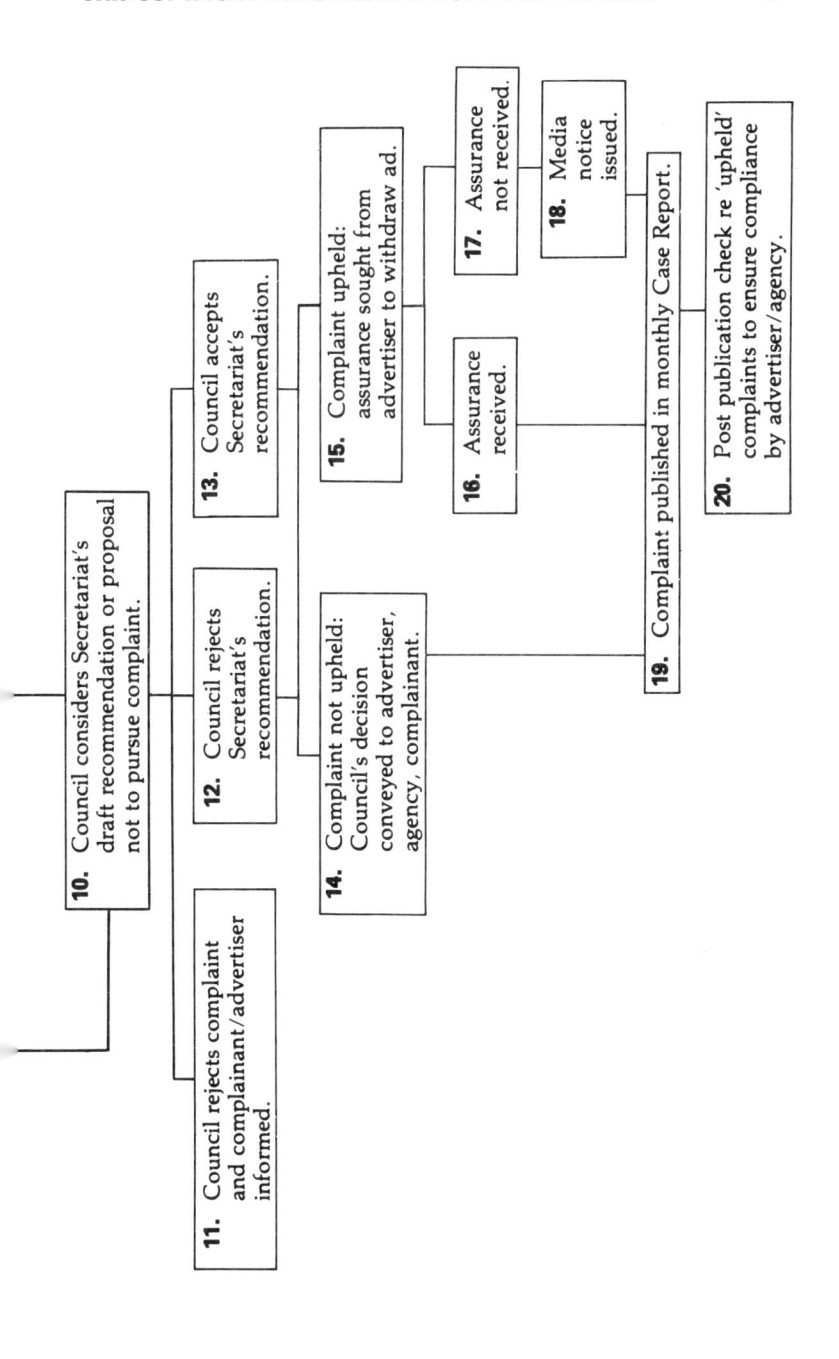

10. Council considers Secretariat's draft recommendation or proposal not to pursue complaint.

11. Council rejects complaint and complainant/advertiser informed.

12. Council rejects Secretariat's recommendation.

13. Council accepts Secretariat's recommendation.

14. Complaint not upheld: Council's decision conveyed to advertiser, agency, complainant.

15. Complaint upheld: assurance sought from advertiser to withdraw ad.

16. Assurance received.

17. Assurance not received.

18. Media notice issued.

19. Complaint published in monthly Case Report.

20. Post publication check re 'upheld' complaints to ensure compliance by advertiser/agency.

CASE 16
YTS, IBM and Saatchi

You can tell a lot about a marketing campaign from its advertisements. The two black-and-white advertisements reproduced in Exhibits 1 and 2 will exercise your skills in evaluating what was attempted and how well it was achieved. They were both produced by Saatchi and Saatchi Compton Ltd as part of larger campaigns for the Manpower Services Commission and IBM. Examine them carefully and be prepared to discuss the following questions:

(a) What basic ideas does the advertisement set out to convey?

(b) What attitudes is the advertisement trying to change?

(c) Who is the target audience?

(d) What emotional appeals does the advertisement make?

(e) In what part of the press would you place the advertisement?

(f) How would you rate this advertisement overall?

Exhibit 1

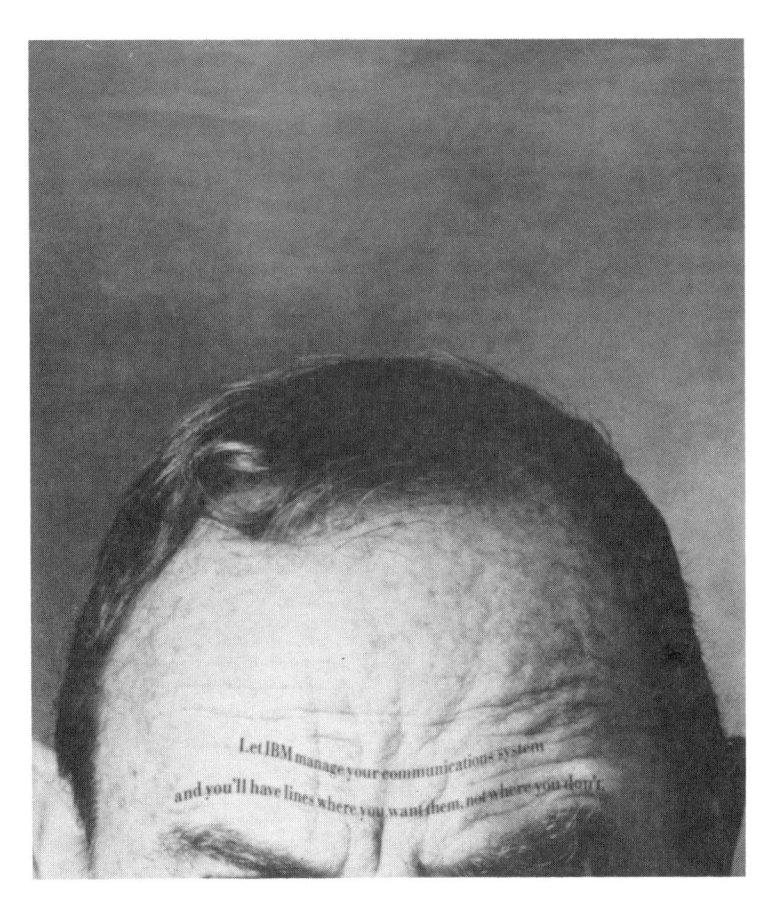

Let IBM manage your communications system and you'll have lines where you want them, not where you don't.

When you use a network service which is managed by IBM, you won't have much to worry about.

You'll have the most highly qualified professionals working for you.

With all the technical resource of IBM behind them.

We will implement and manage a network for your company which works internally, and can link your company to services you need or to other companies in the same field.

We'll install it. We'll maintain it. We'll train your staff to use it.

It's even down to us to keep it in line with the latest technology.

So that when something new comes along, you won't be stuck with equipment you can't use.

To find out more, why not contact Rob Billington, Business Network Services, IBM United Kingdom Limited, 389 Chiswick High Road, London W4 4AL. Telephone 01-995 1441.

All you have to worry about now is finding a pen.   IBM

Exhibit 2

TRAIN THE BIT THAT'S BRITISH AND YOU'LL CHANGE THE WHOLE PICTURE.

You can see what happens when a country doesn't do enough about training its school leavers.

Its young people end up buying other nations' goods instead of making them for themselves.

And whilst Britain has never been short on talent, we have tended to be rather shortsighted on training. We've lagged a long way behind West Germany and Japan for instance, where around 95% of 16 year olds go on to further education or job training.

(Ahem. No need to mention how their economies are doing.)

All is not lost, however. This April, the new 2 Year YTS was born.

And now every 16 year old school leaver in Britain can get two years of first class training – just for the asking. (17 year olds can still train for a year.)

Not only that, over 100,000 of Britain's more far-sighted employers are just waiting to be asked.

The list includes the cream of British business . . . names like Marks and Spencer, ICI and B.P.

(It also excludes hundreds of companies who have so far failed to convince us that they have a proper training scheme.)

Every YTS trainee will have to be given both work experience and off-the-job training.

Definite goals have to be set and met and every training programme will be monitored regularly.

But whilst it's not easy for a company to succeed in getting on the new 2 Year YTS, life will soon be a lot harder for the ones who aren't accepted. Because before long they'll lack the skills they need for the future.

Fortunately, a lot of employers have come to realise that there is a skill crisis in Britain and over 400,000 YTS training places have been promised for this year.

It seems that our school leavers finally have the chance to come up with the goods.

THE NEW 2 YEAR YTS. TRAINING FOR SKILLS.

MSC ACTION FOR JOBS

Pricing

CASE 17
Omega Instrument Ltd

On 12th April 1986, James Lawler, manager of the Automatic Gauging Division of Omega Instrument Ltd, telephoned Roy Brown, plant engineer for the Aerospace Corporation, to advise him of a price he had worked out for an automatic inspection unit. Brown had written to him six days earlier asking Omega to submit a bid for a unit to inspect the machining of a new engine part. Brown's reaction to the '£750,000 or so' quoted by Lawler was that this 'seemed a little high'. He gave no indication of his basis for this statement although Lawler asked why he thought so. Brown avoided the question by saying that he had 'anticipated somewhat less'. Lawler said he would take another look at it and submit the formal written bid in a day or two.

As he put the phone down, Lawler had the distinct feeling that George Turner had also been in touch with Brown. Turner Inspection Co. was Lawler's chief competitor and on three occasions over the past six months had been successful as an alternative bidder to customers Omega had previously served exclusively. On the last occasion, a manufacturer of diesel engines had simply placed a firm order with Turner when Turner had approached them with a lower price after they had seemed to accept Lawler's price offer by telephone. Lawler had never met Roy Brown, but he had spoken to him so many times that Roy would not be surprised at another phone call from Lawler to ask about some technical detail. How, though, could he ask about Turner without giving the show away?

George Turner was a particularly knowledgeable competitor as far as Omega's business was concerned. Until three years ago, he had been Omega's works manager. He had left to set up Turner Inspection Co. shortly after Lawler was appointed manager of the Automatic Gauging Division. At that time, Omega quoted delivery of up to ten months for most orders and International Motor Corporation (IMC), in particular, had been unhappy with this long lead time. Furthermore, they had complained that Omega was favouring their main UK rival. Consequently, they had jumped at the opportunity to finance Turner in return for preferential supply of inspection equipment for their new models. Since then, Turner had taken all IMC's business as well as quite a lot from Omega's customers whenever delivery promises began to creep up. Now, however, deliveries had been pared to the shortest possible time and competition seemed to have become a matter of price.

Lawler was pretty sure that Turner would sooner or later cut his price in order to obtain a first foothold with Aerospace. Turner certainly knew that Aerospace was a big Omega customer. Although Aerospace's purchases from Omega were not evenly spread from year to year, they averaged around £1 million a year with 30% supplied from the Automatic Gauging Division. Turner also would be able to calculate that Omega's price for the current order would be in the £140,000-plus range.

Lawler's price to Aerospace had been based on Omega's standard component-standard price system. This system was the invention of John Fearn, the managing director. A comprehensive range of standard components had been designed as the basic building blocks of all products, both standard and non-standard, sold by Omega's eight divisions. A standard price had been established for each standard component based on the cost of labour, material and machine time required for optimum batch manufacture with full recovery of works cost. On to this figure was added 12½% to recover selling costs and a further 25% of the total to cover profit.

Fearn's philosophy was to establish a 'normal' price for

every order, and to regard this as a target and as a measuring stick for any deviations. Pricing would thus entail merely the addition of the prices for all standard components, plus a small percentage of non-standard work and assembly. Except for an occasional custom-built unit, the non-standard element of an order varied 5% above or below 20%.

Fearn had also extended his approach to standardisation into the control of Omega's divisions. The manager of each of the firm's eight divisions worked to an annual sales and profit target, with the target profit before tax set at 20% of the target sales. The division managers were responsible for obtaining their own orders, for preparing quotations, and for scheduling and supervising production. Idiosyncratic though the approach was, the firm's performance under Fearn's five years of leadership had been outstanding. Omega had increased its output 400% and its employees had grown from 120 to 300.

Up to 31st March, Lawler's division had produced just on 25% of its 1986 target which is shown in Exhibit 1. Orders

Exhibit 1 *Omega Instrument Ltd: Annual Sales and Profit Targets, 1986*

	Automatic Gauging Division (£m.)	Omega Instrument Limited (£m.)
Sales	1.20	10.04
Direct Labour	0.24	2.62
Direct Materials	0.10	1.66
Parts from other Divisions	0.32	—
Variable Overheads	0.06	0.54
Fixed Overheads	0.24	3.20
Total Expenses	0.96	8.02
Profit	0.24	2.02

on hand or pending, however, would not reach more than 75% of normal capacity over the next three months, though they were expected to average the target prices. As there was usually a lead time of around two months in quoting and obtaining an order, Lawler could see little chance of further orders being ready for production before June. The Aerospace unit could fill this gap. If was required by the end of September, which allowed considerably less than the seven months delivery he would normally promise on such an order.

This was the first time since Lawler had taken over the division that he had failed to have a long enough order book to avoid dropping below capacity. Lawler considered that this was not a major recession, just an unexpected lull in demand. Omega had no market research or forecasting unit, but the number of customers to whom Omega supplied automatic units was under fifty, and most of these seemed to be producing at normal levels.

Lawler had quoted the price of the automatic inspection unit for Aerospace based on a standard price calculation of £148,600. This figure included £39,500 plus 20% for parts that would be required from several of the other divisions. These would be charged to Lawler at standard price less the 20% profit, and the supplying divisions' profit targets adjusted to eliminate profit target on inter-divisional work.

In considering the possibility of reducing his price on the Aerospace unit, Lawler was well aware of Fearn's view that no amount of profit-paring was going to make much impression on the price. He should really charge a higher price if he wanted to meet his profit target for the year. Furthermore, Omega had built up a reputation with Aerospace for reliable equipment — exceedingly important for inspection equipment. Omega's installation and servicemen were known to the Aerospace production people and worked well with them and the standard component system had enabled Omega to keep spares without excessive cost and keep repair time to a minimum.

In fact, service might be one area in which Lawler could reduce the price. The price included an allocation of overhead cost for 'debugging' machines and servicing during the first year. It was possible that the Aerospace unit would not require much attention after delivery and that the £6,000 included in the price to cover this cost could be cut out. Also, there was no undertaking to provide this service free.

CASE 18
Construction Industries Ltd

The board of Construction Industries Limited customarily devoted special attention at its February meeting to a review of the group's marketing performance and prospects. The usual accounts and commercial statistics had been circulated with the February 1977 board papers, together with a special five-year forecast by the Commercial Director, Preston Smythe. These are shown in Exhibits 1, 2 and 3. Smythe opened the discussion:

> On the commercial side the group has weathered the deepest recession since the 1930s. The worst is now behind us, however, and I am confident that this year will see us back into profit — provided we keep our production costs under control and restrain overheads. The market is looking a lot healthier than it did two years ago, and we will get the work the production side needs. The commercial side has made its own contribution to efficiency, as can be seen from the comparative statistics, and we intend to keep our staff down to these levels.

Exhibit 1 *Construction Industries Ltd: Group Trading Accounts (£m.)*

	1973	1974	1975	1976
Sales	54	56	58	59
Cost of Invoiced Work	49.1	51.2	53.9	55.3
Gross Margin	4.9	4.8	4.1	3.7
Overheads	3.6	4.2	4.8	4.8
Profit Before Tax	1.3	0.6	(0.7)	(1.1)

Exhibit 2 *Comparative Annual Commercial Statistics (£m.)*

	1973	1974	1975	1976
Order Book at End of Year	35	38	25	20
Orders Received				
Estimated Invoice Value	59.4	58.6	44.9	54.2
Estimated Markup	5.7	5.2	3.0	4.9
Bids Submitted				
Value	331	293	187	285
Estimated Markup Included	33	26	12	26
Enquiries Received				
Estimated Cost of Work	420	338	192	305
Commercial Staff				
(No. of Employees)				
Sales Representatives	11	11	12	10
Estimators	25	24	22	20

Exhibit 3 *Commercial Five-Year Forecast*

Market Conditions
Economic forecasts suggest a very small percentage real growth until 1979, and continued control of government expenditure on new public buildings. Nevertheless, there are some signs of an increase in demand in the sectors in which we operate. Even taking a conservative view we expect a steady growth in the market open to us, as capital expenditure generally rebounds from the small level of orders placed in 1975. Measured in contract cost before margin we estimate the volume of orders that will be placed as follows:

	Last 4 years (actual prices £m.)		Next 5 years (1976 prices £m.)
1973	780	1977	540
1974	600	1978	650
1975	320	1979	725
1976	425	1980	825
		1981	900

Competitive Conditions
There has been a noticeable increase in the average number of

firms bidding against us over the past two years:

Year	1973	1974	1975	1976
Average No. of Competitors	4.0	4.0	4.5	4.6

In our opinion this is a reflection of the smaller volume of new work and we expect that by next year the number will return to its traditional level. As part of our monitoring of competitive conditions, we commissioned a study of competitor prices over the last four years. As far as we can gather there has been only minor variation from year to year in the dispersion of competitor prices on the work we have tendered for. The standard deviation of all bid prices around the average price is around 9.3%. We believe that competitor prices veered downwards by 2 or 3% in 1975, as did ours, but that the competitive lessons have been learned and margins have returned to the old levels. With the hard lessons of recession behind the industry, we predict that margins will gradually creep upwards over the next five years.

Sales and Profit Forecast

Assuming that the economy can be kept on a steady recovery path, the group should be well able to react with a steady increase in orders. Provided that proper precautions are taken to control overhead expenditure, the group should move into substantial profit by 1978. Sales and profit estimates are as follows:

	1977	1978	1979	1980	1981
Orders	75.0	100.0	125.0	150.0	175.0
Markup	7.0	11.0	13.0	17.0	20.0
Overheads	5.2	5.5	5.8	6.0	6.5
Profit Before Tax	1.8	5.5	7.2	11.0	13.5

CASE 19
Baird Roofing

Following its move ten years previously into a single centralised warehouse just off the M1 motorway, Baird Roofing had built itself into the leading producer of flexible roofing materials in the United Kingdom. In the major market segments, Baird had steadily increased its share to 50%. Baird's guarantee of delivery by 8.30 a.m. of all orders received by 5.00 p.m. the previous evening had meant that roofers and builders could virtually eliminate stocks and avoid pilferage and damage. Retailers and merchants could also carry smaller stocks. None of the numerous other manufacturers had their own warehousing and direct distribution organisation, so, except for the occasional direct sale to a large contractor, all used wholesalers for the bulk of their output.

In mid-1986, the steady demand growth for roofing materials began to taper off for the first time in years. Smaller producers started active price cutting to move their production. Baird's philosophy was to lead the industry up and follow it down, so, whenever competitor price reductions were identified, it had countered with similar reductions. By December, prices had declined with four price cuts across the board amounting to 18%. Baird had retained its volume, but with warehouse and fixed manufacturing costs of £18 million and a markup of only $66\frac{2}{3}\%$ on the variable cost of manufacture, profits were already down to only £2 million. Then on 10th December, a major house builder reported that a competitor was offering him yet another 5% price reduction on bitumen-coated flexible roofing.

Assessing the Competition

CASE 20
Albright Ltd

It was August 1980 and plans for the 1981 calendar year were due shortly. The Chairman of the Beta Group had told Graham Peake who managed the Albright subsidiary that he was looking for more profits from Albright. He had a particular concern that the stock analysts would be expecting a good performance as he completed his first four years in office in the following year.

Albright produced a wide range of standard wall switches and sockets for lighting and electrical connections. The principal competitor was Maynard Ltd, which was also the largest and had traditionally led the market in price increases. Eight smaller competitors each held under 10% of the market and had always raised prices when Albright had followed Maynard. Low prices and UK standard specifications effectively ruled out any foreign competition.

Graham Peake had asked for the historical data shown in Exhibits 1 to 5. Because there were so many items in Albright's and Maynard's catalogues, the price of an 'average item' had been calculated by dividing Albright revenue by total number of items. Maynard's average item price had been arrived at by adjusting Albright's for the weighted average price differences in the two catalogues. This had also been reconciled with the estimates of market value and volume and with Maynard's market share and actual revenue figures.

Peake wondered just what he should promise the Chairman.

Exhibit 1 Albright and Maynard: Average Item Prices, Volume and Market Share Estimates — The Historical Pattern

Period Ruling	Competing Average Item Prices (From Price Lists)				Estimated Market Volume (Exhibit 3 Column 2 Adjusted) M. Items	Albright		Maynard	
	Months No.		Albright Average £	Maynard Average £		Sales (Actual) M. Items	Market Share %	Sales (Est.*) M. Items	Market Share %
May 74—Feb 75	10		0.51	0.51	35.2	6.9	(19.6)	14.5	(41.2)
Mar 75—Dec 75	10		0.56	0.56	32.5	6.1	(18.8)	14.2	(43.7)
Jan 76—Jun 76	6		0.60	0.60	19.5	3.5	(17.9)	9.0	(46.2)
Jul 76—Apr 77	10		0.65	0.69	27.2	6.1	(22.4)	8.9	(32.7)
May 77—Jun 77	2		0.69	0.69	6.3	1.4	(22.2)	2.1	(33.3)
Jul 77—Nov 77	5		0.80	0.80	15.8	3.3	(20.9)	5.9	(37.3)
Dec 77—May 78	6		0.87	0.87	19.9	4.0	(20.1)	7.9	(39.7)
Jun 78—Mar 79	10		0.94	0.99	34.1	7.9	(23.1)	10.4	(30.5)
Apr 79—Oct 79	7		1.04	1.05	25.1	5.8	(23.1)	7.7	(30.7)
Nov 79—Mar 80	5		1.19	1.19	18.1	4.0	(22.1)	6.1	(33.7)
Apr 80—Aug 80	5		1.19	1.34	18.3	4.4	(24.0)	5.1	(27.9)

*Maynard Estimate = Market − 3 (Albright Volume).

Exhibit 2 Annual Indicators of Volume and Price

Calendar Year	Index of Construction Output (1970 = 100)	Estimated Industry Volume (1979 = 43m.) (million items)	Wholesale Price Index All Manufactured Output (1980 = 100)
1974	94	43	35
1975	86	39	44
1976	85	39	51
1977	83	38	63
1978	88	40	72
1979	94	43	88
1980 (8 months est.)	95	29	100

Exhibit 3 Albright Limited: Annual Sales, Item Revenue and Market Share

Calendar Year	Sales (£m.)	Profits Before Tax (losses) (£m.)	Volume (million items)	Item Revenue Actual (£)	Item Revenue 1980 Prices (£)	Market Share (%)
1974	4.2	0.4	8.5	0.49	1.40	19.8
1975	4.0	(0.2)	7.3	0.55	1.25	18.7
1976	4.5	(0.3)	7.2	0.63	1.24	18.5
1977	5.8	(0.1)	7.8	0.74	1.17	20.5
1978	8.0	0.4	8.8	0.91	1.26	22.0
1979	10.2	0.2	9.8	1.04	1.18	22.8
1980 (8 mth est.)	8.1	0.3	6.8	1.19	1.19	23.4

Exhibit 4 Maynard Switches Ltd: Annual Sales, Item Revenue and Market Share

Calendar Year	Annual Report Sales (£m.)	Annual Report Profits Before Tax (losses) (£m.)	Volume (Sales Item Revenue) (million items)	Item Revenue Actual* (£)	Item Revenue 1980 Prices (£)	Market Share (%)
1974	9.1	1.9	18.5	0.49	1.40	43.0
1975	9.2	0.9	16.7	0.55	1.25	42.8
1976	8.9	0.3	14.1	0.63	1.23	36.2
1977	8.5	(0.1)	11.2	0.76	1.21	28.9
1978	13.1	1.4	14.1	0.93	1.29	35.2
1979	14.6	0.4	13.8	1.06	1.21	32.1
1980 (8 mth est.)	11.1	N.A.	8.7	1.28	1.28	29.7

*Exhibit 1 adjusted to Calendar Year Basis

Exhibit 5 *Maynard Switches Ltd: Summary of Accounts*

	1979 (£m.)	1978 (£m.)
Turnover	14.6	13.1
Profit before Taxation	0.4	1.4
Taxation	0.2	0.7
Dividend	0.4	0.4
Current Assets		
Cash	0.4	0.4
Debtors and Pre-payments	2.2	1.8
Stocks	3.3	2.8
	5.9	5.0
Less Current Liabilities		
Bank Overdraft	3.5	2.4
Creditors	1.3	1.6
	4.8	4.0
Net Current Assets	1.1	1.0
Fixed Assets	3.2	3.4
Total	4.3	4.4
Financed by:		
Debentures and Loans	2.7	2.6
Shareholders' Funds	1.6	1.8
	4.3	4.4

CASE 21
Ciba-Geigy*

In early 1986, the management of Ciba-Geigy UK was confronted with the need to decide a strategy for facing future competition against its leading ethical drug, Voltaren. The patent protecting Voltaren in the UK was due to expire in April 1986 and they were concerned that there might be a repetition of Ciba-Geigy's experience following the expiration a year earlier of the West German patent on the Voltaren molecule. During 1985, Voltaren had lost 50% of its volume in Germany to low-priced generic equivalents. As one magazine commented, 'Given that the ingredients of a well-established product usually cost only a few pennies, it can be seen that there is virtually a "no-win" situation facing a company when a product's patent expires. It usually comes down to playing a losing hand brilliantly'.

Voltaren was Ciba-Geigy's leading ethical drug with worldwide sales in 1985 of about $445 million out of a total corporate turnover of $10.2 billion. It was used to alleviate pain and reduce swelling from rheumatism and other musco-skeletal diseases — technically termed a non-steroidal anti-inflammatory drug (NSAID).

The pharmaceutical market in the United Kingdom was valued at £1,500 million in 1985 and the NSAID segment represented just under 11% of this figure. The bulk of the NSAID demand went to six branded products as follows:

---

*This case has been prepared from published sources.

Company	Drug	1985 Market Share
Ciba-Geigy	Voltaren	16%
Syntex	Naprosyn	15%
Pfizer	Feldene	15%
Boots	Brufen	9%
M.S.D.	Indocid	9%
Lederle	Lederfen	8%

Voltaren was priced 5% above the others but even so was gaining market share at 1% a year.

Competition between the different brands of NSAID was based largely on the two qualities of effectiveness and gentleness. Effectiveness was a measure of a brand's efficacy in reducing pain or swelling. Gentleness was an inverse measure of the frequency and severity of side effects. Voltaren ranked high on both measures. Doctors tended to believe, however, that no product could be both highly effective and very gentle. Producers' marketing teams, therefore, tended to emphasise one attribute or another. Ciba-Geigy placed the emphasis on Voltaren's gentleness relative to Pfizer's Feldene.

After the product's patent expired, the brand name would protect the drug to some extent. Doctors mostly prescribed by brand name. Ciba-Geigy, however, could only raise advertising and sales promotion expenditure above 6% of sales if it were prepared to pay a UK Government levy of 100% on any excess. This had been imposed in order to limit the amount the National Health Service paid for producers' efforts to orient its spending towards their own product.

Direct sales to hospitals accounted for 20% of the physical volume sold. Branded NSAIDs sold to hospitals were already heavily discounted. Hospitals required the producers to submit price tenders in order to get their brand onto the list of drugs that each hospital authorised its staff to prescribe. The price levels were as low as 60% of the price charged to retail. Once started on a prescription by a hospital, however, a patient would normally continue with the same brand after returning home.

In addition to the leading brands, just under 10% of the market in value and nearly 20% in volume of prescriptions were supplied by generic compounds. These percentages were growing, and were double the 1984 levels. Generic products had the same chemical composition as the branded products, but of course none was yet based on the Voltaren molecule.

Generic producers avoided the research cost of developing and testing drugs and also the promotion cost of establishing them in general use. If the experience in the United States and Germany were to be repeated, however, generic producers would not cut prices too drastically except in the hospital sector. Generally speaking, they seemed to look to the longer term. In any case, after 1990, there would be fewer patents expiring, and generic producers seemed to want to develop lines protected by their own brand names. In the UK, branded generics were already being marketed directly to doctors, and several companies were also developing new ways of administering generic drugs to patients, such as 'patch' release or one-per-day tablets. Competition was thus moving away from a clear-cut conflict between research-based producers and generic producers. In the UK, Glaxo, a world leader in research-based pharmaceuticals, had already set up a quasi-generic unit to sell pharmaceuticals under a 'GX' brand label. Glaxo had backed up this GX unit with a field force of 30 representatives, which was a good size even for a conventional research-based manufacturer.

CASE 22
Henshall Confectionery

Among Peter Avery's duties at Henshall Confectionery was responsibility for the Vendomatic account. Since the Christmas break ten weeks previously when Peter took over the account, the account performance had been disappointing. Sales had slipped by nearly 20% on the previous year and the contribution of £6,000 for the ten weeks looked decidedly sick.

Vendomatic held the franchise from the Transport Authority for stocking the automatic chocolate vending machines on the Authority's premises. Special chocolate packs were supplied to Vendomatic by both Henshall and its major competitor, Pastile, at a standard price agreed annually with the Vendomatic and Transport Authority management. The price allowed a commission to Vendomatic on the volume sold and a royalty to the Transport Authority. From time to time, the vending machine price to the customer could be adjusted but, given the mechanical limitations of the machines, the bulk of the adjustment was made by the confectionery companies with changes in the quantity of chocolate in the packs.

The vending machines contained either three or five slots with two allocated to chocolate — one for a Henshall pack and one for a Pastile pack. Henshall's and Pastile's brands were advertised widely with high public brand awareness and both firms offered a milk chocolate, a plain chocolate and a nut and raisin chocolate. Vendomatic, however, was not prepared to stock the machines with more than one brand at a time from each competitor. Their staff servicing the machines would, they claimed, be involved in unnecessary costs if they had to carry more than two chocolate lines. Staff frequently had to carry supplies up and down escalators in use and for a considerable distance along corridors. Furthermore, they would need to spend more time packing in their vans if they had multiple brands from each supplier. The agreement reached was that each supplier would supply one of its brands each week and could change the brand for the Monday delivery.

Exhibit 1 *Henshall and Pastile Brand and Volume Returns*

	Henshall		Pastile		Total
Week	Brand	Packs (000s)	Brand	Packs (000s)	Packs (000s)
1	Plain	17.2	Milk	17.2	34.4
2	Nut	15.3	Plain	18.7	34.0
3	Plain	19.7	Nut	16.0	35.7
4	Milk	15.9	Nut	19.5	35.4
5	Plain	14.9	Milk	20.2	35.1
6	Milk	14.8	Plain	18.0	32.8
7	Nut	17.9	Plain	14.6	32.5
8	Milk	18.9	Nut	15.3	34.2
9	Nut	14.4	Milk	19.5	33.9
10	Plain	19.4	Milk	14.2	33.6
	TOTAL	168.4		173.2	341.6

Each Monday, Vendomatic provided both competitors with a return showing for each the brand used in refilling the machines during the preceding week and the quantities placed. These returns for the past ten weeks are shown in Exhibit 1. While nut chocolate represented the smallest placements for Henshall's, Peter Avery calculated that, if he eliminated nut chocolate altogether in favour of plain chocolate, he could increase the £6,000 contribution for the ten weeks by a further £500. With the added requirements of its manufacture, nut chocolate remained the most expensive, even after adjustment of the chocolate and nut content.

Contributions for the ten weeks were:

	Packs (000s)	Contribution Per Pack	£
Plain	71.2	4.0p	2,848
Milk	49.6	3.6p	1,786
Nut	47.6	3.0p	1,428
	168.4		6,062

Controlling the Marketing Function

CASE 23
Southern Steel Fabricators

At the annual strategy conference for Southern Steel Fabricators, a marketing presentation showed that the company had completely lost its position in the market for steel motorway bridges. In fact, all steel suppliers had lost out to suppliers of pre-cast, reinforced concrete girders. Discussion convinced the directors that they were not losing out on price, but rather on speed of delivery and in the convenience of incorporating standard construction units into motorway specifications.

The concrete firms provided the motorway design engineers with catalogues of their standard girders complete with full measurements and details of load bearing, stress testing, and standard price. All the design engineer had to do was to design to the standard and specify a number. For steel bridges, however, the designer had to specify to the steel supplier's sales force what was required. The steel firm then drew up designs and submitted them for approval, along with a price quotation. Once an order was approved, a requisition for the steel was placed on the rolling mills and the steel company could then confirm the delivery date — allowing for the necessary fabrication and drilling.

In order to reverse their competitive failure, it seemed to the Southern Steel Board that they should appoint an executive to take responsibility for steel road bridges. Nobody seemed to have much idea, however, where they would find such a person. Furthermore, Southern was functionally organised with design management, works management, sales management, purchasing and finance and accounting functions. Where would such an executive fit, and how would he interact with these functions?

CASE 24
Tony Sheehan

'I have four alternatives, but I really don't know which is best. I could look for a job in another company, I could confront George Baker, I could ask Alastair Thomson for clarification of my responsibilities, or I could sit tight and wait for developments'. Tony Sheehan, marketing director of British Continental Brands (BCB) of London, was mulling over the frustration of his new position as he sat over dinner with his wife.

Sheehan, aged 40, had been headhunted three months previously by an executive search firm working for the BCB chairman, Alastair Thomson. Thomson had wanted to get the best, most up-to-date practitioner of the marketing of packaged consumables that the headhunters could find. He had felt for some time that the BCB organisation tended to slip away from attention to its consumer markets and to pursue its brand marketing as though it were an age-old ritual. He wanted someone who would pull the organisation up to the frontiers of marketing practice.

A substantial increase in salary had succeeded in enticing Tony Sheehan from his position as UK marketing director for an international beverage firm. Moreover, BCB offered him a real challenge with its worldwide turnover approaching £2 billion and high and consistent profits — although with very little growth. At the same time, there was almost no central marketing input. Management of BCB's national sales subsidiaries was controlled from the small holding company headquarters largely through budget planning and review sessions run by the triarchy of BCB's chairman, managing director and finance director. Although subsidiary

97

performance in terms of volume growth and market share achieved was considered at the budget meetings, marketing details were not required. The same was true for the brand-owning subsidiaries. These companies produced and sold their products largely through the national sales subsidiaries, although in some cases they sold direct to outside distributors and in other cases they licensed a larger sales subsidiary to manufacture on their behalf. Some of these brand-owning subsidiaries employed international brand managers. They operated at arm's length from the sales subsidiaries and any influence they exercised over the sales activities was based on the weight of the particular case they presented, not on any organisational power.

Alongside Tony, and also reporting directly to Thomson, was George Baker, the international brand coordinator. Baker, aged 53, had been with BCB for many years. He worked primarily with the management of the brand-owning companies to stimulate development and testing of new brands and their worldwide release. He was also involved with issues concerning the management and rejuvenation of existing brands. While George had been warm and welcoming to Tony, he had not provided him with any details of his current activities and concerns. George never volunteered to talk to Tony about brands and all brand correspondence came directly to George.

Only the day before, Tony had learned from a group circular that George had organised and run a Worldwide Brand Managers' Conference in Rome two weeks previously. When Tony had asked for a summary of the proceedings, George stated blandly that they had not kept minutes in that sense. Tony had begun to feel that George had expropriated the job of the marketing director, leaving him with nothing but some central public relations budget.

CASE 25
Tinsley Crouch Ltd

Shirley Jones worked in the West End as personal secretary to Doreen Wright, a product line manager for Tinsley Crouch Ltd. The firm specialised in developing flavours and fragrances for new consumer products and Ms. Wright travelled a great deal to visit customers and suppliers and to attend conferences. Shirley normally arranged her boss's tickets through a call to nearby travel agents who sent an invoice to Tinsley along with the tickets. The invoice was signed by Ms. Wright and then went to the accounts section for payment.

One day in May 1983, Shirley was handed a copy of *Ms. London* as she left the tube station. Reading it over coffee, Shirley came across the following feature and accompanying advertisement (Exhibit 1):

Token of Gratitude
IF YOU'RE a secretary who makes a lot of travel bookings for your boss, then The Business Travel Centre want to attract your custom. So much so that they're offering Marks & Spencer Gift Vouchers for every booking made, to the value of about $2\frac{1}{2}$ per cent of the cost of the booking. In practical terms this means if you book a flight to Paris you'll get a voucher of £3; for a booking to Melbourne you'll get about £50. Apparently this amount does not push up the price of the ticket, but is taken out of BTC's commission. They have a motorbike messenger who'll deliver the tickets.

The Business Travel Centre is at 52 Manchester St, W1 (935 3840).

Exhibit 1

FREE GIFT VOUCHERS

THE BUSINESS TRAVEL CENTRE

52 Manchester Street,
London W1M 5BP.
Telephone: 01-935 3840.

THE SPECIALISTS IN BUSINESS TRAVEL

SECRETARIES! P.A.'s!
Book your boss's next business trip
with us to receive
Marks & Spencer Gift Vouchers.
Offer valid to 30 September 1983.

Extract from *Ms London*, Monday 9th May 1983.

The idea of gift vouchers seemed very attractive to Shirley. She was finding London costs particularly oppressive at this time. In fact, she literally could not make ends meet. Unemployment had kept wage increases in check, but not British Rail fares. Not only that, her flatmate had just left and Shirley now had to go through all the pains of finding and adjusting to an entirely new flatmate in a one-bedroom flat. Despite all her secretarial qualifications, a flat of her own seemed further away than ever, let alone the luxury of ever running a car.

Shirley showed the advertisement to Elizabeth Holmes, the financial director's secretary in the next office. Elizabeth thought the idea terrific, too. They both agreed that the firm might possibly obtain a discount if it pooled travel purchases with one travel agent — but as it had not done so, the vouchers would not be taking anything from the firm. They were pretty sure, too, that the porter on the front desk took a kick-back from the taxi firm — and that a clerk in charge of stationery did very well from 'gifts'.

Shirley called up The Business Travel Centre to ask if there were any need to register for the scheme and how long it would last. The girl on the other end said she only needed to mention it when she called in a booking: 'We've had such a terrific response we are going to keep it going beyond September'.

Shirley wondered whether she should ask her boss's permission.

CASE 26
British United Breweries

As Greg Moran passed the telephonists' office in British United headquarters, he was tempted to burst in and give them a piece of his mind. He was considerably annoyed about the treatment he had received earlier in the day when calling in to his secretary. He had had to wait for about 25 rings before his call was answered by an unintelligible 'British United'. He had then been unceremoniously switched through to the extension he asked for while he was still in mid-sentence and about to ask that as he was using a pay phone, could he have a second extension if the first was busy. To cap it all, his secretary was apparently out of the office, the operator did not come back on the line, and he had used his last coins.

Greg was national sales manager for the firm's nationally-advertised beer brand and was responsible for some 350 representatives working out of regional sales offices. Although few customer enquiries came directly to the head office, some did. Furthermore, Greg believed telephone presentation to outsiders was important for other functions as well — not least for marketing management who also worked at headquarters.

Earlier in the year, Greg had written a memorandum of complaint to the director of administration to whom the six telephonists reported. All that he had achieved was a long explanation of how difficult it was to cope with this problem. The director claimed that at no reasonable salary could they attract reliable and trainable people simply to answer telephone calls all day. Greg's suggestion that all executives should have their own direct line and that calls would revert to the central exchange only if the direct line were not answered did not appeal at all. The director of administration pointed out that there was no saving to justify the added overhead and he would have no argument to place before the finance director.

Greg did not himself want to make a pitch to take over administration of telephones, but he knew they had no problems with telephonists in the regional sales offices.